SandCastle™

Baby
African Animals

It's a Baby
Gazelle!

Kelly Doudna

Consulting Editor, Diane Craig, M.A./Reading Specialist

ABDO
Publishing Company

Published by ABDO Publishing Company, 8000 West 78th Street, Edina, Minnesota 55439.

Printed in the United States.

Editor: Liz Salzmann
Content Developer: Nancy Tuminelly
Cover and Interior Design and Production: Mighty Media
Photo Credits: Ablestock, Digital Vision, Eyewire, Getty Images (Gerald Hinde), iStockPhoto (Sebastien Burel, Rick Parsons), Peter Arnold Inc. (Michel & Christine Denis-Huot, Malcolm Schuyl, A. Shah), ShutterStock

Library of Congress Cataloging-in-Publication Data

Doudna, Kelly, 1963-
  It's a baby gazelle! / Kelly Doudna.
     p. cm. -- (Baby African animals)
  ISBN 978-1-60453-153-4
1. Gazelles--Infancy--Juvenile literature. I. Title.

  QL737.U53D68 2009
  599.64'69139--dc22

                          2008005470

SandCastle™ Level: Fluent

SandCastle™ books are created by a team of professional educators, reading specialists, and content developers around five essential components—phonemic awareness, phonics, vocabulary, text comprehension, and fluency—to assist young readers as they develop reading skills and strategies and increase their general knowledge. All books are written, reviewed, and leveled for guided reading, early reading intervention, and Accelerated Reader® programs for use in shared, guided, and independent reading and writing activities to support a balanced approach to literacy instruction. The SandCastle™ series has four levels that correspond to early literacy development. The levels are provided to help teachers and parents select appropriate books for young readers.

Emerging Readers
(no flags)

Beginning Readers
(1 flag)

Transitional Readers
(2 flags)

Fluent Readers
(3 flags)

SandCastle™ would like to hear from you. Please send us your comments and suggestions.
sandcastle@abdopublishing.com

Vital Statistics

for the Gazelle

BABY NAME
fawn

NUMBER IN LITTER
1 to 2, usually 1

WEIGHT AT BIRTH
6 to 14 pounds

AGE OF INDEPENDENCE
1½ years

ADULT WEIGHT
26 to 165 pounds

LIFE EXPECTANCY
10 to 15 years

A mother gazelle is called a doe. She cleans her newborn fawn.

Fawns lay completely still in the grass. This makes it harder for predators to see them. The mother gazelles graze nearby.

Half of all gazelle fawns are killed by predators.

The mothers return to nurse their fawns three or four times each day.

Many animals prey on gazelle fawns. Cheetahs are the only animals able to run fast enough to catch adult gazelles.

Cheetahs can run fast only for short distances.

Gazelles live in herds
on plains and grasslands.
A herd may have hundreds
of gazelles.

Gazelles are herbivores. Zebras and wildebeests eat the tall grass. Then gazelles graze on the short grass that is left over.

Gazelles stot when they are scared by a predator. Stotting is running slowly and then leaping straight up in the air. Then they run away.

Scientists think that a gazelle stots to show how healthy it is.

Gazelles stamp their front feet and snort to signal danger.

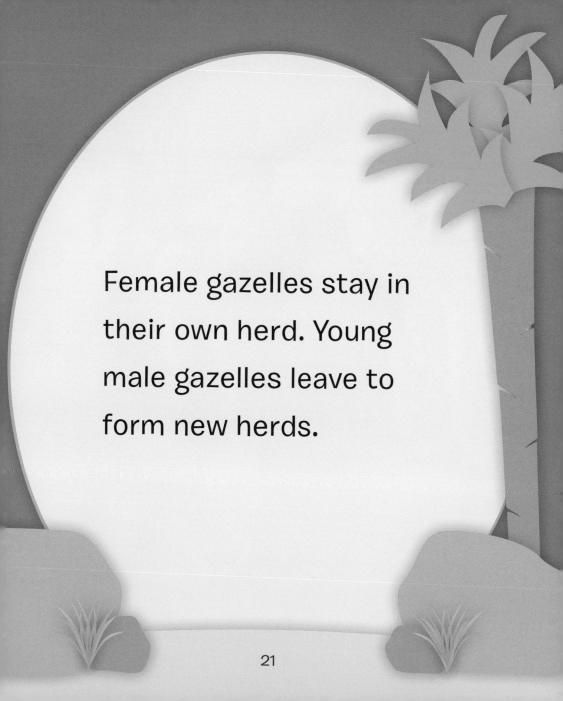

Female gazelles stay in their own herd. Young male gazelles leave to form new herds.

Fun Fact

About the Gazelle

When stotting, a gazelle leaps 10 feet into the air. That's higher than the ceilings in many houses.

10 feet

Glossary

ceiling – the upper surface or lining of a room.

expectancy – an expected or likely amount.

grassland – a large area of land covered with grasses.

graze – to eat growing grasses and plants.

herbivore – an animal that eats mainly plants.

independence – no longer needing others to care for or support you.

nurse – to feed a baby milk from the breast.

plain – a large, flat area of treeless land.

predator – an animal that hunts others.

prey – to hunt or catch an animal for food.

signal – to send a message using a sound, sign, or device.

snort – to make a short, loud noise by breathing out suddenly through the nose.

To see a complete list of SandCastle™ books and other nonfiction titles from ABDO Publishing Company, visit **www.abdopublishing.com**.

8000 West 78th Street, Edina, MN 55439

800-800-1312 • 952-831-1632 fax